Four Hundred and Two Snails

Haiku Society of America
Members' Anthology
2018

Nicholas M. Sola, Editor

All prior copyrights are retained by contributors. Full rights revert to contributors upon publication in the Member's Anthology. The Haiku Society of America, its officers, and the Anthology editor assume no responsibility for the views of any contributors whose work appears in the Anthology, nor for research errors, infringement of copyright, nor failure to make proper acknowledgment of previously published material.

ISBN-13: 978-1-930172-18-0

Listed in the MLA International Bibliography, Humanities International Complete, and Poets & Writers.

© 2018 by the Haiku Society of America, Inc.

Layout: Ignatius Fay

Front cover: Utagawa Hiroshige (Ando) (Japanese, 1797-1858). *New Fuji, Meguro, No. 24 in One Hundred Famous Views of Edo*, 4th month of 1857. Woodblock print, Image: 13 7/16 x 9 in. (34.1 x 22.9 cm). Brooklyn Museum, Gift of Anna Ferris, 30.1478.24 (Photo: Brooklyn Museum, 30.1478.24_PS1.jpg).

Back cover: Utagawa Hiroshige (Ando) (Japanese, 1797-1858). *Original Fuji, Meguro, No. 25 in One Hundred Famous Views of Edo*, 4th month of 1857. Woodblock print, Image: 13 5/8 x 9 in. (34.6 x 22.9 cm). Brooklyn Museum, Gift of Anna Ferris, 30.1478.25 (Photo: Brooklyn Museum, 30.1478.25_PS1.jpg)

Introduction

In 2018, the Haiku Society of America celebrated its fiftieth anniversary. To honor the occasion, members were asked to submit their five best haiku for inclusion in the twenty-fifth annual members' anthology. All members who submitted by the deadline have one poem in this anthology.

I must thank every member who submitted their work for this anthology. I would also like to thank everyone who supported and helped me with this anthology, especially Fay Aoyagi, Ignatius Fay, Dianne Garcia, David Lanoue, Michelle Murchie and Bri Whetstone. Finally, I must thank you, the reader. Of all the books you could be reading right now, you picked this one. May it be worthy of your time.

Nicholas M. Sola
Editor

hard to see
in designer camouflage
a baby

Deb Koen

trickster wind
a beach ball
travels the coast

Lynne Jambor

halyards in the breeze
Sunday morning bells
calling their flock

Adelaide B. Shaw

stained glass
a shaft of sun drowns out
the soprano

    Antoinette Libro

strategically placed
in the garden of eden –
leaves

    Dana Grover

minister thunders
enumerating our sins
jackdaw cawing

    Bob Whitmire

baby feeding herself…
that little mouth
so hard to find

    Carolyn M. Hinderliter

street fair
he counts out my change
in his mother tongue

    Stephen Colgan

bone-in unicorn steak
just the taste of that thought

    Thomas Chockley

outdoor cafe
a stiff breeze carries
river scent

Angelee Deodhar

nothing to spend
a pocketful
of broken sand dollars

C.J. Prince

antacid …
do anteaters
get heartburn

David J Kelly

carousel
i reach for the brass ring
and miss

    Renee Londner

old slave market:
two black boys buying
cotton candy

    L. Teresa Church

Chopin prelude
after the music
cardinal echoes

    Christina Laurie

rain drumming all day search for a rhythm

Jeff Stillman

foothills -
the lumps and bumps
of grandma's shoes

Ann Rawson

clear
through the open skylight
the neighbor boy's song

Ruth Yarrow

from a roller coaster
the thrill
of a sunset

Mykel Board

end to the weekend…
the steam rises
pressing my white shirt

Charlotte Digregorio

Looking skyward —
millions of years to make nights
partially safe

Bruce England

just remember
it's all a simulation
spaceship windows

    Charles Harmon

Florence by night
in 1704
the paint still wet

    Peter Meister

the day after
the same lake
darker

    Susan B. Auld

just one new car
how to get it
back on the shelf

    Bryan Hansel

road hum
our elbows touch
and touch

    Barbara Hay

mountain trip
the uncertainty
behind the curves

    Klaus-Dieter Wirth

silken hair
brushing my lips
her coquettish smile

    Tom Lyon Freeland

the babbling brook
bubbles along to the sea
leaf boats float away

    Gerald A. McBreen

the towhee peers
down a gopher hole
whodunnit weather

    Dian Duchin Reed

his kiss lingers
on my lips –
cotton candy

    Frances Greenhut

cupped cheeks
the tattered globe
on two poles

    Srinivasa Rao Sambangi

when bubbles touch
a fragile affair
clearly

    Ann M. Penton

strangers talk about
players and scores
solar eclipse

      Nancy Shires

windy afternoon
all eyes
on the bagpiper's kilt

      Christopher Herold

hidden in everything plain sight

      Don Wentworth

kookaburra
the catchy ripples
of a laugh

Marietta McGregor

afternoon stroll
even the wildflowers
have hairy legs

Bob Oliveira

biggest fish
of the day
Vincent's tall tale

Carolyn Noah Graetz

bouncing raindrops
my fingers still tapping
the ukulele tune

Jacquie Pearce

too many
broken covenants
zoo cages

Jackie Maugh Robinson

rocky shore—
the footprints that couldn't
be found

Roy Kindelberger

an empty envelope
her boyfriend
of seven years

Michael Roach

starless night
could wishing
be enough

Lydia T. Liu

blue moon
i write four haiku
in a dream

Scott Glander

To mention that
The cat is sleeping
Seems redundant

michael mathews

inner workings of a clock
last night's dream with
a complex plot

John J. Han

coffee spill
I butt-dial
Laos

David G. Lanoue

Above the refrigerator
Even here
Dog hair

    William E. Lee III

on the wild side —
a monarch slips
across the border

    Dan Curtis

quiet rain
my signature
in his guestbook

    Barbara Tate

every flake
is different
call-in radio

LeRoy Gorman

deep well
the doubt in the echo
of my shout

George Swede

marriage proposal
by haiku
 she counts syllables

Roberta Beach Jacobson

the places
where dreams slip in…
my studio door ajar

Rebecca Drouilhet

aspen wind
we applaud the dance
of the deaf girl

Sarah E. Metzler

their life
in a plastic bag
the line of Rohingya

Miriam Borne

overnight case…
crammed with jewelry
for more than overnight

    Sidney Bending

    political ads
    back again
    asparagus ferns

        M. Franklyn Teaford

    before
    the tripwire
    after

        William Scott Galasso

trousseau
he dresses her
in fingerprints

    Margaret Rutley

pond ripples…
the coyote lapping up
its reflection

    Keith Polette

merging clouds --
we rewrite our dreams
in the daisies

    Julie Warther

                    contrails
                    the lines
                    he snorts

                            Raymond Roy

at river's edge
another special stone
I leave in place

        Peggy Bilbro

            No wine
            No vice
            Loner's life

                    Manoj Mathur

late night bottle
how our rocking
becomes a prayer

Tia Haynes

arrhythmia the unraveling of the republic

Bruce H. Feingold

night border crossing
new hope in America
mother and her son.

Jason Scott Wallace

dawn sky
I look away from
the green light

    Jim Laurila

railroad crossing—
the many arms
that kept me safe

  Kendall Lott

crossing a street
against the wind
I'm nearly at a standstill

    Paulette Y. Johnston

long, thin raindrops fall
framed by gray city canyon
jewels in this light

    Shasta Hatter

on my wrist
bead by bead
time passes

    Lidia Rozmus

break room
everyone operating
a device

    Lori Becherer

slanting sunlight i have her mouth

frances angela

gentrification
exposed tree roots
hold a stone

Robert Forsythe

#MeToo
the changing colors
of the seasons

Lori Zajkowski

deep in the cave the silence of our flashlights

Ben Moeller-Gaa

we both hate peas wedded bliss

Denise Fontaine-Pincince

lunch hour
a man in a tie
fishes from a bridge

Jeffrey Ferrara

farewell bow
the river between us
rushes on

    Jennifer Thiermann

hovering over
bills that must get paid
hummingbird

    James Won

in the crowd
umbrellas drip
elbow to elbow

    Edward J. Rielly

rumble of the metro
a queue of city crabs
inches forward

Fay Aoyagi

waiting for you
I slip the family photo
from its frame

kjmunro

home from errands—
a hero's welcome
from the dog

Annette Makino

twilight deepens I call my sons in

Carmen Sterba

late at night
rock star
out to lunch

Marita Gargiulo

jet lag a pocketful of pounds

Tanya McDonald

rain through the night again the dream of chewing glass

          David Boyer

busy morning—
the bottle with the last drop
in the trash

          Gary Hotham

arrivals
my son's
stubble

          David Jacobs

Ancestral home—
Wall to wall every corner
Whispers my childhood

    VeerajaR

beetle spots
the nicknames
we never outgrow

    Michelle Schaefer

family reunion
he longs for
closed captioning

    Marilyn Powell

home again—
the sparrows fill me in
on the gossip

Michelle Heidenrich Barnes

post-vasectomy,
this 'primal' urge
to overpunctuate

Lew Watts

kitchen gadgets
mother forgets the names
of her daughters

Nika

Department of State
old white sycamore
leans into traffic

    Kristen Lindquist

On the way to golf
I saw migrant laborers
working in a field.

    Daniel A. Zehner

clouds ride with me…
 dad's second stroke

  Karen O'Leary

raindrops on blacktop
obscure bright flashing white lines
snorted by lost souls

Andy Felong

his first time
sporting a beard
rehab hospital

Sheila Sondik

disorderly conduct the wildflower wind

Francine Banwarth

free-range bobcat
spotted near farmhouse –
one less chicken

Donna Pohlmann

broken window
I save
all the pieces

Kath Abela Wilson

those final years
the drool on dad's shirt
a droplet on my journal

Diane Wallihan

lying in disgrace
in rain covered gutter--
broken umbrella.

    John S. Gilbertson

piano casters…
the last notes
leave the house

    Alan S. Bridges

highest bidder at the auction adjusts her signet ring nightfall

    Francis Attard

starless sky
the black cord
to the fuse box

Robbie Coburn

long haul
the conversation dwindles
into snores

Madhuri Pillai

Apache tears
one more mother lights up
the night sky

Robert Epstein

morning doorbell
it is never
you again

    Bill Pauly

Savannah row house
coquettish despite decay--
disheveled lady

    Jonathan Bowman

old Brownie photo
my smiling parents
before me

    Sue Colpitts

river wind
the sting
of sulfur rain

    Chris Bays

fat cat
mouse tail
nothing more

    John Budan

bus terminal----
an old man
savors his popcorn

    Julia Cousineau

tapestry of clouds
swirling and superimposed
at the rotary

Mary Weidensaul

over 55
putting the recliner
in reverse

Brenda Lempp

paintings of trees
on old pine walls
quiet music

Ellen Grace Olinger

leaving the garden
my mother takes with her
the Latin names

susan spooner

in her library
an empty tea cup,
a closed book

Patricia Harvey

antique shop
everything older
than I am

Dorothy McLaughlin

pecking order of sparrows —
my grandson raises his hand

    Jim Sullivan

rain on the marsh
swollen fingers
find the chords

    Glenn G. Coats

fallow field—
the wild side
of old exotics

    Charlie Shiotani

cliff dwellings
from a crumbling wall
a crow watches us

    Frank Higgins

maple leaf
dancing in the wind
game over

    Rick Jackofsky

Same old excuses
my heart is a no-show

    Merle Burgess

Ahhhh home!
Long solo hours
Stretch before me.

Claudia Updike

it begins in the distance
a blue powder in the canyon air
dusk

Marshall Hryciuk

windswept night
we put ourselves
on mute

Joan Prefontaine

balancing act
the last thread of reason
escapes him

    Bona M. Santos

stormy night
only in my dream
do I return fire

    Perry L. Powell

Saturday morning rain…
a driving lesson
with my father

    Stanford M. Forrester

memories
forty years of road maps
in the recycle bin

    Gretchen Graft Batz

ironing
where did all these wrinkles
come from

    Donna Bauerly

story of my life
she tears it apart
with commas

    Sondra J. Byrnes

borrowed time -
I put more honey
in my tea

      Anita Curran Guenin

end of season
the tiger mascot
begins chemo

    Merle Hinchee

basket of blueberries…
counting change
his hands tremble

    Elizabeth Howard

in the desk drawer
the yellowed ticket
to visit you in Paris

Frank Judge

elderberry jam
jars memories
of my youth

E. Luke

old dreams revealed
Elvis at the senior center

Judith Hishikawa

bridge game
every hand
liver spotted

Terri L. French

nursing home garden
the Kansas wind tousles
his thin hair

Randy Brooks

funeral plans
even here
economies of scale

Roger Watson

enduring ailment…
her husband loosens
his wedding vows

    Robin Smith

just widowed
all she accomplishes
without him

    Claire Vogel Camargo

funeral luncheon
the crescent shape
of a bone dish

    Susan Godwin

paupers' cemetery
only the clouds
come and go

    Sharon Rhutasel-Jones

the ruined graveyard
toppled stones and dank litter
old majestic trees

    David Cashman

where everybody knows your name tombstone

    Robert B McNeill

emerald fingers
stretching to embrace nighttime
calm tangerine clouds

    Judith M. Vance

rustling leaves
the hedgehog bristles
in darkness

    Joanna Ashwell

after midnight
the faraway moan
of a freight train

    Dean Summers

old metronome—
where time
now rests

    Michael J. Galko

new year
a tumbleweed pauses
and drifts right

    Padma Thampatty

white world in wild winds
the one fair sun repelling
when Persephone rose

    D Perez

first day of spring--
dad browses through
the hospice handbook

    Ruth Holzer

snowdrops
at the old place
bloom for someone else

    Mary Frederick Ahearn

past lives -
that butterfly
looks familiar

    Jeannie Martin

small feet
scamper thru the field
spring fever

K.O. Smith

the warmth
of her mother tongue
first crocus

Bryan Rickert

lingering at the rest stop a frog's eggs

Eric Burke

Dandelion
Under my chin
- she runs away

Mark Hitri

In the card
on Valentine's Day…
ultrasound

George Skane

spring moon
a teacup
full to the brim

Natalia L Rudychev

first redwing
Allen Brook
turns a corner

Elizabeth Hazen

open to suggestion
I choose
the rosebud

Michele Root-Bernstein

Spring rain
  a sprinkle of arpeggios
    from the street musician

Sylvia Forges-Ryan

a hyacinth
in her chipped cup —
hospice room

 Marion Alice Poirier

Utah sky painted ladies flying north

 Johnnie Johnson Hafernik

trailing arbutus
I kneel to breathe in
the spring mountain

 John Quinnett

sandy footprints
already gone behind me
hazy horizon

    Agnes Eva Savich

after rain
a warm breeze wringing
all 'round dry

    Ellen Peckham

the way he looked back
yet again –
spring fever

    Elizabeth Bodien

cool light of late snow early morning jazz

Beverly Acuff Momoi

bridge's shadow
tree swallows sweep
into my thoughts

Anne Elise Burgevin

first star...
she strains
to find the kite

Randall Herman

my orange peel
brightens the forest floor
leave no trace

Bruce Ross

a speck of light
in the catbird's eye
magnolia in bloom

Craig Kittner

not quite ready
to release the sorrow…
remaining snow

Michael Sheffield

frog song
the brightest stars
are first

 Roland Packer

popping up
in the usual places
spring haiku

 Rick Tarquinio

skunk cabbage
down by the brook
my soul rejoices

 Merrill Gonzales

          heads turning
          at the air show
          a butterfly

                  Dennise Aiello

dandelion seed
drifts past in brilliant sunlight
that thought I lost

      Art Elser

        O power sublime
        triggering an avalanche
        fluttering wings

              CE Gallagher

migrating geese --
the things we thought we needed
darken the garage

    Chad Lee Robinson

above the trees
a mountain has melted
into haze

    Michael McClintock

bubbles rise
in garden spring
nightingale song

    Ron LaMarsh

ephemeral white
blossoms of tears
magnolia's joy

Frances Farrell

as though the tree's soul
has fled
wild bees

Stuart Bartow

the last patch of snow
melted in my pocket
Route 66

Sharon Lynne Yee

first kiss
as husband and wife…
lilacs in full bloom

    Elinor Pihl Huggett

spring light—
I might take
the backroad

    Mary Hanrahan

Meditation Point
fronds uncurl
to learn their shape

    Dianne Borsenik

jeweled stained glass panes
land on cardinal flowers
butterfly chapel

    Christine Wenk-Harrison

thirty year old gift
Holland tulip bulbs
friendship in bloom

    Maureen Lanagan Haggerty

the kite's pull—
   in another life I wore
a braided pigtail

    Barry George

springtime carousel
the melody
of horses

Fred Andrle

cherry blossom
a bar regular vents
his spleen

Stella Pierides

the blue sky
would have been enough
cherry blossoms

Susan Beth Furst

middle of april
the same unopened boxes
in a new corner

mark larkspur

willow moon
shamisen notes drift
over the canal

Leanne Mumford

cherry blossoms
cover me sleepin' self
Guinness Stout

Thomas Dougherty

spent blossoms—
the remission, too,
was unexpected

    Mary Kendall

scribbled dreams
on an index card
spring cleaning

    Bob Lucky

Texas flannel—
soft yellow stars
in full bloom

    Janis Albright Lukstein

songbirds chirp
in unison
which smoke detector is it?

    Tami M. Johnson

spring haze
a squirrel at the zoo
in foot traffic

    Cyndi Lloyd

out of the chipper the cherry's golden heartwood

    Connie Hutchison

sunshowers…
he buries his mouse
in the marigold patch

    J Hahn Doleman

a yellow-bellied marmot
nibbles Indian paintbrush
the road to Yellowstone

    Judy Duncan

artesian spring
a childhood memory
out of nowhere

    Sam Bateman

after the consult
an uneasy stillness …
thunderstorm watch

Julie Bloss Kelsey

a fork in the road …
I stop
for a robin's song

Chen-ou Liu

declaration form—
I eat a cucumber
in the airport toilet

John S Green

sunken doorways
   taut leaves play tag
with decaying children

       Paul Sleman Clark

words scroll
on the plasma tv
summer night

      Lenard D. Moore

shape shifts
neurons change
color coded octopus

      Carole Slesnick

beer garden
the skip and hop
of hailstones

Hans Jongman

second inning
the sound of one man
napping

James A. Paulson

Mother's Day
her apron
now her bib

Patricia Rogers

laughing dove
the rhythm of
my heart sutra

Matthew Caretti

painting calla lilies
her brush lingers
in the shadows

Mark Forrester

small town lights
on the desert horizon
flower moon

Judith Morrison Schallberger

lawn mower -
squirrel sits on the fence
twitching his tail

    Lee Strong

May sunshine
on the wooded path
the sparkle of his eyes

    Deanna Tiefenthal

knock knock
an unknown caterpillar
on a common weed

    Carolyn Coit Dancy

summer breeze
the widow next door
starts dating

Cherie Hunter Day

starflowers
light the woodland…
we find our way

Debbie Strange

she lets me think what i like lapwing

Jim Kacian

old photos:
sixty miles from the ocean
surfboards on the van

Steven H. Greene

a bit of something
falls from a tree
summer heat

Seren Fargo

crash of thunder
the cat follows the dog
under the bed

Patricia Prine

city pond--
bullfrogs reply
to the policeman's bullhorn

    RaNae Merrill

old dog's cough
the color of
strawberries

    Sharon R. Wesoky

the radon seared lungs
my uncle gave for his country
Memorial Day

    Gregory Longenecker

hollyhocks
I wish I had such
good posture

Michael Fessler

still pond
a turtle pokes his nose
through a cloud

Laurie D. Morrissey

Beach Vacation

Waves surge to the shore
over seashells on the beach
effervescent sound

David Patten

waterfall
the streak of grey
in my wife's hair

Rob Grotke

making love
i seek your eyes
summer lightning

Arch Haslett

desert wind
the chimes you gave me
sound hollow

Kathryn Bold

green moss
draws faces
granite boulders

    John-Carl Davis

Summer-
the loneliness of a bus driver
on a Sunday afternoon.

    Anthony Franco

pour me
mosquito wines
in my ear

    Warren Decker

week of rain
the birdbath
empties itself

George Dorsty

summer car wash
the toddler soaping
her belly first

Dyana Basist

humid night
social affair –
strange fruit

Harold Cowherd

hollyhocks blooming
hummingbird sampling nectar
barbed wire fence

Wilma McCracken

still proudly displayed
the Fathers' Day pencil box
on my crowded desk

Barth H. Ragatz

another dove nestling
hits the dust
ah, Darwin

Doris Lynch

afternoon thunderstorm
beach plans
washed away

      Joette Giorgis

into a mound
lifeguards rake footprints
from the sand

      Jeffrey McMullen

a trace of salt
on the back of her neck
Midsummer's Eve

      Marilyn Fleming

her first
shoebox funeral
midsummer sun

Amelia Cotter

sandspit
egrets bicker
over territory

Erica Ison

zucchini blossom
just this once
i let her wear the bling

Jennifer Hambrick

tin cones
fringe a dancer's kilt
summer rain

Victor Ortiz

running for its life
the fence lizard takes a leap
to the other side

Aubry Hemingway

abalone shell
in my hand
the sunset's afterglow

Lesley Anne Swanson

mailman arrives
I'll take a rain check-
broke summer.

 Kendra E. Shaw

reminding me
to slow down
turtle crossing

 Robin White

by the fire hydrant
a single hollyhock
spilling its seeds

 Margaret Chula

on grooming day
she gets a July 4th bow
my puppy fast asleep

    Ida Freilinger

the comfort woman
sends the Lord of Date off—
summer bird's call

    Tadao Okazaki

thunder without rain
saying just enough
then stopping

    Mariam Kirby

tomatoes [if ripe]
good wine [if cheap]
friends over for dinner

Nancy Bright

cactus bud
her old story
takes a new twist

Katherine Raine

catfish where our mythologies differ

Lorin Ford

promises
we never keep
summer wind

    Frank J. Tassone

climbing season
the breath-taking view
from the loo

    J. Zimmerman

the tinkling
of her jade bangles…
jasmine blossoms

    Theresa A. Cancro

a language
full of questions
mourning doves

Brad Bennett

the square root
of zero…
summer clouds

Angela Terry

moving closer
to the dying campfire
pine knot

Ken Olson

lavender …
when need and want
are one

    Mimi Ahern

        bullfrog's rhythmic groan -
        the sound of grandmother's chair
        on her wooden porch

            Robert K Keim

        drought
        my ears have lost
        the creek

            Sandi Pray

watermelon truck
my father's madras shirt sleeves
clinging to his arms

Sari Grandstaff

in no rush
to settle down
the milkweed seed

Pat Davis

face in the cradle
of the old massage table
motionless spider

Scott Wiggerman

electrical storm
our lips touch
but don't take hold

Mary Weiler

amid the stones
of the soldiers' cemetery
edelweiss

S.M. Kozubek

last light of day
one cicada drowns out
the interstate

Michael Henry Lee

waning summer
even prayer
is not enough …

Amy Losak

on the fringe of autumn—
the blue door
to hot yoga

Vicki McCullough

summer's end—
dust gathering on books
I planned to read

Kathe L. Palka

last day of summer
the pocket jingle
of chosen shells

    Michele L. Harvey

my lost golf ball
and the alligator…
summer ends

    Jo Balistreri

mistakes
may have been made…
kudzu

    Stephen Amor

backyard feeder
    migrant birds
        welcome here

Karen DiNobile

oars still
I dip my sleeve
into the cupped moon

Connie R Meester

each mindful crease
        of the origami crane
    August morning

Michael Dudley

rock wall ivy
the child clings
to her father's hand

Dianne Koch

long night
I crawl inside
a love poem

Dan Schwerin

jumbled fish nets
a woman blesses the harvest
by kissing a salmon

Richard Tice

a temple in ruins
a lover waits too long—
pale moonlight

Clarise Samuels

this one kiss
from head to toe
ocean moon

John Hawk

super moon
the stars
advise patience

Stephanie Lemmons Wilson

lost power —
only the moon charging
my devices

Suzanne Niedzielska

flash of color
  in morning dew -
    hummingbird.

Jim Bloss

yoga class
we sit quietly together
after the hurricane

Howard Lee Kilby

his goodbye—
the sun too
lost in fog

Jill Lange

his turn to cook
again he can't find
the thyme

Caroline Giles Banks

crescent moon
sometimes faith is all
that is left

d w skrivseth

shooting stars—
the wine we cooled
among the river stones

    Ellen Compton

Morning drizzle
dragonflies dancing
on the surface of the lake

    Joseph Fulkerson

off to college
my child
and checkbook

    Daniel J. Geltrude

new moon
my optometrist
out of options

Brent Goodman

autumn rain
the lost light
of leaves

Ann K. Schwader

small talk
the creek scampers
beyond its banks

Marilyn Ashbaugh

my lifeline
against the redwood stump
morning mist

Billie Wilson

white cloud
flies by—
covey of quail

Gil Jackofsky

after the hurricane leaf blowers

Robyn Hood Black

crickets
the pulse in a hollow
of her neck

    Tom Painting

    almost
    a full moon
    this romance

        Ronald K. Craig

    evening sky-
    construction crane shimmering
    with starlings

        Sue Mackenzie

full moon…
waves gather
in silver wrinkles

    Steve Tabb

        the poet speaks
        out the window
        the full moon

            Barbara Ungar

Full moon dawn
A squirrel travels from
   branch to branch
along the horizon.

    Marci McGill

deep into autumn
the curl
of a panhandler's hand

Sharon Pretti

purple chicory
a calf's ear catches
the wind

Anna Cates

waning moon
the wine bottle covered
with candle wax

Skaidrite Stelzer

one tale
leads to another
fall constellations

     Kathryn J. Stevens

slipping in
behind the other guests
autumn wind

     Patricia J. Machmiller

in the truck
with the seat belt buckled
my prize pumpkin

     Marilyn Appl Walker

rising tide
all my best fishing
runs through it

Marcyn Del Clements

September night
the loons'
last songs

Patricia Nolan

yellow ginkgo leaves
with stems every which way
a walk with mom

Jon Hare

steam engines
at the county fair
she sighs

Eric Arthen

clouds baffle
  a slivered moon
news of a suicide

Patricia McKernon Runkle

on the same last note
played on the violin
the geese come in—honking

Rick Clark

slow lava
evermore pungent--
long night

brett brady

autumn air
an old friend's voice
on the radio

Matthew Moffett

scattered clouds
the sky stitched
with geese

Joseph Robello

hare's moon
the few embers
that linger

Alan Summers

a steady stream
of fences
refugee moon

Renée Owen

blood moon —
young lions roar
just for practice

Lysa Collins

splitting the sky
one deep crimson vein
evaporates the moon

    Erin Castaldi

day moon …
ghosts of half-remembered
dreams

    Joanne M. Reinbold

after she leaves
the weight
of hanging apples

    Marsh Muirhead

cat eyes
out in the black night
a falling star

    Devin Harrison

fog settles on the river
the stories
they didn't tell us

    Valorie Broadhurst Woerdehoff

fallen cone
from the sugar pine
broken clouds

    Deborah P Kolodji

sleepless night   dewdrops on the weeds

Ludmila Balabanova

Canada geese—
I was only taught to draw
them flying away

Tom Sacramona

prayers for the dead
float on the wind
October sunset

John G. Bernth

first frost—
a rust colored feather
in the bluebird box

Mike Stinson

winter rain
I practice walking up the stairs
backwards

Alison Woolpert

<u>Crimson Red</u>
A bottlebrush tree
Unique and beautiful
As red as crimson

Alison Finch

seasoning her onion soup
these ancient tears
in the mixing bowl

Susan Boyle

winter ridgeline
a long drawn-out conversation
with wind

Mark Dailey

Veteran's Day
he burns the candle
both ends

Juliet Seer Pazera

cold spell
iguanas
falling from trees

    Mike Schoenburg

            frost moon
            the silver platter
            I didn't polish

                Holli Rainwater

        winter sunrise
        butter finds its own path
        across grandma's skillet

            Frank Hooven

the last words
I didn't hear her say
first leaf to fall

Ignatius Fay

the drawstring missing
from my hoodie ...
blustery day

Connie Donleycott

one blond strand winter sunlight

Bill Gottlieb

leaf fall
the sheet of rain
over granite

    Dianne Garcia

orion moves
out of the window frame
fresh start

    Alanna C. Burke

winter blues —
the harmonica man plays
for Wall Street

    Don Baird

Thanksgiving--
our future daughter-in-law
brings a new dish

Anna Eklund-Cheong

christmas lights
all that there is
to see by

Patti Niehoff

winter morning
I wonder if those tears
were about a boy

Susan Antolin

simmering—
chicken noodle soup
and a cold

    Mike Montreuil

night frost—
I watch the valet
wreck my car

    Crystal Simone Smith

russet raincoat pushing
perambulator through leaves
chin jutting toward some future

    Tom Hahney

missing mitten--
my granddaughter asks
if I need help

    Gary Evans

second honeymoon
the electric blanket
set on high

    Joe McKeon

silent night
only a winter moon
interrupts the stars

    Wanda D. Cook

time to go
a dried leaf falls
from my passport

> *Olivier Schopfer*

knife blade
skin curls circle
onion tears

> *Marian M. Poe*

depth of winter
the ukulele just right
in my arms

> *Karina M. Young*

ghost images
settling dusk
on a withered branch

    Robert Sorrels

frost warning tonight
in the garden
we say goodbye

    Elizabeth Martens

winter solstice
the backyard chickens
take themselves to bed

    Vanessa Proctor

these Christmas lights —
how I wish my children
were still small

Lynn Edge

year's end
I leave my clothes
on the floor

Barbara Snow

peeling clapboards
a snow flake settles
on the pink flamingo

Bill Deegan

winter stars—
a kiss
on the old school bus

Nicholas M. Sola

snow falls
on evergreens
boxes in the attic

Robert Witmer

cold sheets
on half the bed
she remembers

Jone Rush MacCulloch

in the middle of the storm snow angels

    Sneha Sundaram

ice covers stone
names on monument
seek higher power

    Eileen Sateriale

wind-driven snow--
a dipper's song
carried downstream

    Paul Hendricks

wolf moon …
all you have left
is your magic

    Bonnie Stepenoff

fresh tracks
in the snow～
new stories

    Joan Chaput

graceful long necks
against grey stormy skies
trumpeters

    Robert Bruntil

snow globe
the perfect day
to stay inside

Peter Newton

Crowning a thicket
of stark winter privet
a red cardinal

De Pascuale

deepening debt—
snow along the rim
of the clay flower pot

Michael Dylan Welch

sliding across ice
_____a page of ink
slurs

Jean Aldriedge

seaside grave -
a humpback whale
breaks the surface

Gregory Piko

edge of spring
the shovel sharpened
down to bright steel

Robert Gilliland

Publication Credits

Ahearn, Mary Frederick. "snowdrops" *Acorn*, no. 40, Spring 2018.
Ahern, Mimi. "lavender..." *Frogpond*, vol. 41, no. 1, 2018.
Amor, Stephen. "mistakes" *The Heron's Nest*, vol. XIX, no. 4, December 2017.
Andrle, Fred. "springtime carousel" *Presence*, no. 58, 2017.
angela, frances. "slanting sunlight" *The Heron's Nest*, vol. XVIII, no. 1, March 2016.
Aoyagi, Fay. "rumble of the metro" *Mariposa*, no. 23, 2009.
Arthen, Eric. "steam engines" *New England Letter*, no. 48, 2014.
Ashbaugh, Marilyn. "small talk" *Modern Haiku*, vol. 48, no. 1, 2017.
Auld, Susan B. "the day after" *Acorn*, no. 38, Spring 2017.
Baird, Don. "winter blues—" *The Wonder Code*. Ed. Scott Mason. 2017.
Balabanova, Ludmila. "sleepless night" *Modern Haiku*, vol. 43, no. 3, 2012.
Balistreri, Jo. "my lost golf ball" *Prune Juice*, Feb. 2018.
Banks, Caroline Giles. "his turn to cook" *Midwest Haiku Anthology*, 1992.
Banwarth, Francine. "disorderly conduct..." *Frogpond*, vol. 40, no.3, 2017.
Bartow, Stuart. "as thought the tree's soul" *Akitsu Quarterly*, Summer 2017.
Basist, Dyana. "summer car wash" *Geppo*, vol. XLII, no. 3.
Bateman, Sam. "artesian spring" *Mayfly*, no. 64, 2018.
Bays, Chris. "river wind" Honorable Mention Award Winner, Irish Haiku Society International Haiku Competition, 2017.
Becherer, Lori. "break room" *cattails*, October 2017.
Bending, Sidney. "overnight case..." *Haiku Canada Review*, vol. 10, no. 1, February 2016.
Black, Robyn Hood. "after the hurricane..." *Modern Haiku*, vol. 49, no.1, 2018.
Bold, Kathryn. "desert wind" *Modern Haiku*, vol. 49, no. 2, 2018.
Boyer, David. "rain through the night..." *Modern Haiku* vol. 48, no. 1, 2017.
Burke, Eric. "lingering..." *Modern Haiku*, vol. 48, no. 2, 2017.
Byrnes, Sondra J. "story of my life" *Modern Haiku*, vol. 47, no. 2, 2016.
Cates, Anna. "purple chicory" *Frogpond*, vol. 39, no. 2, 2016.
Coburn, Robbie. "starless sky" *Windfall*, no. 6, 2017.
Compton, Ellen. "shooting stars—" *Presence*, no. 55, 2016.
Cotter, Amelia. "her first" *Now This: Contemporary Poems of Beginnings, Renewals, and Firsts*. 2013.
Dailey, Mark. "winter ridgeline" *tinywords*, vol. 17, no. 1, 2017.
Dancy, Carolyn Coit. "knock knock" *Frogpond*, vol. 38, no. 3, 2015.
Davis, Pat. "in no rush" *Akitsu Quarterly*, Spring 2018.

Deegan, Bill. "peeling clapboards" *The Heron's Nest*, vol. XVII, no. 2, June 2015.

Digregorio, Charlotte. "end to the weekend…" *Asahi Haikuist Network*, March 3, 2017.

Doleman, J Hahn. "sunshowers…" *Acorn*, no. 40, 2018.

Donleycott, Connie. "the drawstring missing" *The Heron's Nest*, vol. XX, no. 1, March 2018.

Dudley, Michael. "each mindful crease" *The Heron's Nest*, vol. XX, no. 2, June 2018.

Edge, Lynn. "these Christmas lights—" *Chrysanthemum*, no. 18, Oct 2015.

Eklund-Cheong, Anna. "Thanksgiving—" *Acorn*, no. 40, Spring 2018.

Fargo, Seren. "a bit of something" *Modern Haiku*, vol. 46, no. 1, 2015.

Feingold, Bruce H. "arrhythmia" *Mariposa*, no. 36, 2017.

Ford, Lorin. "catfish" *Under the Basho: One Line Haiku*, December 2017.

Forges-Ryan, Sylvia. "Spring rain" *Take a Deep Breath*. Kodansha International, 2002.

Forrester, Mark. "painting calla lilies" *Frogpond*, vol. 37, no. 1, 2014.

French, Terri L. "bridge game" *Prune Juice*, no. 7, Winter 2012.

Furst, Susan Beth. "the blue sky" *Presence*, no. 60, 2018.

George, Barry. "the kite's pull—" *The Heron's Nest*, vol. IV, no. 6, 2002.

Godwin, Susan. "funeral luncheon" *HUMMINGBIRD*, vol. XXVI, no. 1, 2016.

Gorman, LeRoy. "every flake" *Haiku Canada Review*, vol. 12, no. 1, February 2018.

Gottlieb, Bill. "one blond strand" *Frogpond*, vol. 41, no. 2, 2018.

Green, John S. "declaration form—" *Clover, A Literary Rag*, vol. 14, Winter 2017.

Guenin, Anita Curran. "borrowed time—" Sharpening the Green Pencil 2017 - contest publication.

Hambrick, Jennifer. "zucchini blossom" *Frogpond*, vol. 40, no. 2, 2017.

Hanrahan, Mary. "spring light—" *Hedgerow*, no. 123, 2018.

Harmon, Charles. "just remember" *Haiku Windows: Spaceship Windows*, June 6, 2018.

Harvey, Michele L. "last day of summer" Kaji Aso Haiku Contest Honorable Mention, 2018.

Haslett, Arch. "making love" *KoKaKo*, June 2011.

Hatter, Shasta. "long, thin raindrops fall" *Haiku Journal*, no.46, 2016.

Hawk, John. "this one kiss" Honorable Mention, Robert Frost Haiku Contest, 2012.

Haynes, Tia. "late night bottle" *Blithe Spirit*, vol.28, no.1, 2018.

Hendricks, Paul. "wind-driven snow—" *Modern Haiku*, vol. 47, no. 2, 2016.
Herold, Christopher. "windy afternoon" *The Heron's Nest*, vol. XX, no. 1, 2018.
Higgins, Frank. "cliff dwellings" *Frogpond*, vol. XVI, no. 1, 1993.
Hishikawa, Judith. "old dreams revealed" *New England Letters*, no. 82, February 2018.
Hooven, Frank. "winter sunrise" *The Heron's Nest*, vol. XIX, no. 1, 2017.
Hotham, Gary. "busy morning—" *Shearsman Magazine*, no. 50, Spring 2002.
Hryciuk, Marshall. "it begins in the distance" *The Asahi Shimbun*, May 1, 2005.
Huggett, Elinor Pihl. "first kiss" *Stardust*, February 2018.
Jacobs, David. "arrivals" *Modern Haiku*, vol. 49, no. 2, 2018.
Jambor, Lynne. "trickster wind" *Earthsigns*. Eds. Michael Dylan Welch and Scott Wiggerman. Press Here, 2017.
Jongman, Hans. "beer garden" *Below the frost line*. catkin press, 2017.
Judge, Frank. "in the desk drawer" *Frogpond*, vol. 41, no. 2, 2018.
Kacian, Jim. "she lets me think..." *after/image*. Red Moon Press, 2017.
Kendall, Mary. "spent blossoms—" Vancouver Cherry Blossom Invitation 2017, USA Sakura Awards, Honorable Mention.
Kilby, Howard Lee. "yoga class" *World Haiku Review*, no. 10, 2008.
Kirby, Mariam. "thunder without rain" *Frogpond*, vol. 41, no. 2, 2018.
Kolodji, Deborah P. "fallen cone" *Plum Tree Tavern*, August 20, 2017.
Kozubek, S.M. "amid the stones" Second prize, 21st Mainichi Haiku Contest, International Section.
Lange, Jill. "his goodbye—" *Mayfly*, no. 62, Winter 2017.
larkspur, mark. "middle of april" *yesterday's sunset*. turtle river press, 2016.
Libro, Antoinette. "stained glass" *The Haiku Calendar* 2018, Snapshot Press.
Losak, Amy. "waning summer" *Asahi Haikuist Nework*, September 29, 2017.
Lott, Kendall. "railroad crossing—" *Modern Haiku*, vol. 49, no. 2, 2018.
Lucky, Bob. "scribbled dreams" *Modern Haiku*, vol. 49, no. 1, 2018.
Luke, E. "elderberry jam" *Geppo*, vol. XXXVIII, no. 3, 2013.
Lukstein, Janis Albright. "Texas flannel—" *Mariposa*, vol. 38, 2018.
Machmiller, Patricia J. "slipping in" *Modern Haiku*, vol. 48, no. 1, 2017.
Makino, Annette. "home from errands—" *Modern Haiku*, vol. 44, no. 1, 2013.
McClintock, Michael. "above the trees" *Shinzouokudou*, no. 1, 2004.
McCullough, Vicki. "on the fringe of autumn—" *Haiku Canada Review*, vol. 10, no. 1, 2016.
McGregor, Marietta. "kookaburra" *Hedgerow*, no. 123, 2018.
McNeill, Robert B. "where everybody..." *Modern Haiku*, vol 49, no. 2, 2018.
Meester, Connie R. "oars still" *KoKaKo*, no. 28, 2018.

Metzler, Sarah E. "aspen wind" *Modern Haiku*, vol. 49, no. 1, 2018.
Moeller-Gaa, Ben. "deep in the cave…" *ephemerae*, no. 1A, 2018.
Momoi, Beverly Acuff. "cool light…" *Frogpond*, vol. 41, no. 2, 2018.
Montreuil, Mike. "simmering—" *bottle rockets*, vol 19, no. 2.
Moore, Lenard D. "words scroll" *Acorn*, no. 39, Fall 2017.
Morrissey, Laurie D. "still pond" *Frogpond*, vol. 41, no. 2, 2018.
Mumford, Leanne. "willow moon" *9th Yamadera Basho Memorial Museum English Haiku Contest: Selected Haiku Submissions Collection*, 2017.
Muirhead, Marsh. "after she leaves" *Frogpond*, vol. 34, no. 3, 2011.
Newton, Peter. "snow globe" *Otata*, no. 16, March 2017.
Ortiz, Victor. "tin cones" *The Heron's Nest*, vol. 20, no. 1, 2018.
Owen, Renée. "a steady stream" *Modern Haiku*, vol. 48, no. 2, 2017.
Packer, Roland. "frog song" *Presence*, no. 58, 2017.
Painting, Tom. "crickets" *Acorn*, no. 10.
Palka, Kathe L. "summer's end" *paper wasp*, vol. 16, no. 3, 2010.
Paulson, James A. "second inning" *Frogpond*, vol. 36, no. 3, 2013.
Pauly, Bill. "morning doorbell" *Mayfly*, no. 62, 2017.
Pierides, Stella. "cherry blossom" *Sonic Boom*, no. 3, 2015.
Piko, Gregory. "seaside grave—" *Modern Haiku*, vol. 49, no. 1, 2018.
Pray, Sandy. "drought" *The Heron's Nest*, vol. XIX, no. 3, 2017.
Pretti, Sharon. "deep into autumn" *Mariposa*, no. 31, 2014.
Prine, Patricia. "crash of thunder" *Modern Haiku*, vol. 46, no. 1, 2015.
Raine, Katherine. "cactus bud" *still heading out: An anthology of Australian and New Zealand haiku*. paper wasp, 2013.
Rainwater, Holli. "frost moon" Honorable Mention, Autumn Moon Haiku Contest, 2016.
Rawson, Ann. "foothills—" *Blithe Spirit*, vol. 27, no.4, 2017.
Reed, Dian Duchin. "the towhee peers" *Akitsu Quarterly*, Fall 2017.
Rhutasel-Jones, Sharon. "paupers' cemetery" *Modern Haiku*, vol. 48, no. 1, 2017.
Robello, Joseph. "scattered clouds" *Acorn*, no. 38, 2017.
Robinson, Chad Lee. "migrating geese—" *The Heron's Nest*, vol. XIII. no. 1, 2011.
Rutley, Margaret. "trousseau" *Erotic Haiku—Of Skin On Skin*. Eds. George Swede and Terry Ann Carter, 2017.
Sacramona, Tom. "Canada geese—" *Asahi Haikuist Network*, October 21, 2016.
Schopfer, Olivier. "time to go" *Under the Basho: Modern Haiku*, 2015.
Schwader, Ann K. "autumn rain" *Modern Haiku*, vol. 49, no. 1, 2018.

Shiotani, Charlie. "fallow field—" *Frogpond*, vol. 37, no. 3, 2014.
skrivseth, d w. "crescent moon" *Modern Haiku*, vol. 48, no. 2, 2017.
Snow, Barbara. "year's end" *Frogpond*, vol. 38, no. 1, 2015.
Sondik, Sheila. "his first time" *bottle rockets*, no. 30, 2014.
Stevens, Kathryn J. "one tale" *Modern Haiku*, vol. 48, no 3, 2017.
Stillman, Jeff. "rain drumming" *Acorn*, no. 34, 2015.
Stinson, Mike. "first frost—" *The Heron's Nest*, vol. XX, no. 1, 2018.
Strange, Debbie. "starflowers" 2017 Snapshot Press Haiku Calendar Competition.
Summers, Alan. "hare's moon" *Mainichi Shimbun*, October 27, 2017.
Swanson, Lesley Anne. "abalone shell" *a hundred gourds*, vol. 4, no. 4, 2015.
Swede, George. "deep well" *Presence*, no. 58, 2017.
Tassone, Frank J. "promises" *Failed Haiku*, vol. 2, no 21, 2017.
Tate, Barbara. "quiet rain" *Modern Haiku*, vol 49, no. 1, 2018.
Walker, Marilyn Appl. "in the truck" Senryu/Haiku Third Place Award, Croatia Pumpkin Festival, 2016.
Wallace, Jason Scott. "night border crossing" *The Asahi Shimbun*, August 18, 2017.
Watts, Lew. "post-vasectomy," *Modern Haiku*, vol. 48, no. 2, 2017.
Wentworth, Don. "hidden…" *tinywords*, vol. 13, no. 2, 2013.
Wilson, Kath Abela. "broken window" *Wales Haiku Journal*, Spring 2018.
Woerdehoff, Valorie Broadhurst. "fog settles on the river" *Modern Haiku*, vol. 49, no. 1, 2018.
Won, James. "hovering over" *What The Wind Can't Touch: Southern California Haiku Study Group Anthology 2016*.
Woolpert, Alison. "winter rain" *Mariposa*, no. 37, 2017.
Yarrow, Ruth. "clear" *Acorn*, no. 38, 2017.
Young, Karina M. "depth of winter" *Mariposa*, no. 36, 2017.
Zajkowski, Lori. "#MeToo" *Frogpond*, vol. 41, no. 2, 2018.
Zehner, Daniel A. "On the way to golf" *Philadelphia Says: Haiku*. Philadelphia, The Moonstone Press, 2018.

Index of Poets

Ahearn, Mary Frederick	59	Boyer, David	35
Ahern, Mimi	99	Boyle, Susan	124
Aiello, Dennise	68	brady, brett	118
Aldriedge, Jean	138	Bridges, Alan S.	41
Amor, Stephen	103	Bright, Nancy	96
Andrle, Fred	73	Brooks, Randy	54
angela, frances	30	Bruntil, Robert	136
Antolin, Susan	128	Budan, John	44
Aoyagi, Fay	33	Burgess, Merle	48
Arthen, Eric	117	Burgevin, Anne Elise	65
Ashbaugh, Marilyn	110	Burke, Eric	60
Ashwell, Joanna	57	Burke, Alanna C.	127
Attard, Francis	41	Byrnes, Sondra J.	51
Auld, Susan B.	12	Camargo, Claire Vogel	55
Baird, Don	127	Cancro, Theresa A.	97
Balabanova, Ludmila	122	Caretti, Matthew	81
Balistreri, Jo	103	Cashman, David	56
Banks, Caroline Giles	108	Castaldi, Erin	120
Banwarth, Francine	39	Cates, Anna	114
Barnes, Michelle Heidenrich	37	Chaput, Joan	136
Bartow, Stuart	70	Chockley, Thomas	7
Basist, Dyana	89	Chula, Margaret	94
Bateman, Sam	77	Church, L. Teresa	9
Batz, Gretchen Graft	51	Clark, Paul Sleman	79
Bauerly, Donna	51	Clark, Rick	117
Bays, Chris	44	Clements, Marcyn Del	116
Becherer, Lori	29	Coats, Glenn G.	47
Bending, Sidney	24	Coburn, Robbie	42
Bennett, Brad	98	Colgan, Stephen	7
Bilbro, Peggy	26	Collins, Lysa	119
Black, Robyn Hood	111	Colpitts, Sue	43
Bloss, Jim	107	Compton, Ellen	109
Board, Mykel	11	Cook, Wanda D.	130
Bodien, Elizabeth	64	Cotter, Amelia	92
Bold, Kathryn	87	Cousineau, Julia	44
Borne, Miriam	23	Cowherd, Harold	89
Borsenik, Dianne	71	Craig, Ronald K.	112
Bowman, Jonathan	43	Curtis, Dan	21

Dailey, Mark	124
Dancy, Carolyn Coit	82
Davis, John-Carl	88
Davis, Pat	100
Day, Cherie Hunter	83
Decker, Warren	88
Deegan, Bill	133
Deodhar, Angelee	8
De Pascuale	137
Digregorio, Charlotte	11
DiNobile, Karen	104
Doleman, J Hahn	77
Donleycott, Connie	126
Dorsty, George	89
Dougherty, Thomas	74
Drouilhet, Rebecca	23
Dudley, Michael	104
Duncan, Judy	77
Edge, Lynn	133
Eklund-Cheong, Anna	128
Elser, Art	68
England, Bruce	11
Epstein, Robert	42
Evans, Gary	130
Fargo, Seren	84
Farrell, Frances	70
Fay, Ignatius	126
Feingold, Bruce H.	27
Felong, Andy	39
Ferrara, Jeffrey	31
Fessler, Michael	86
Finch, Alison	123
Fleming, Marilyn	91
Fontaine-Pincince, Denise	31
Ford, Lorin	96
Forges-Ryan, Sylvia	62
Forrester, Stanford M.	50
Forrester, Mark	81
Forsythe, Robert	30
Franco, Anthony	88
Freeland, Tom Lyon	14
Freilinger, Ida	95
French, Terri L.	54
Fulkerson, Joseph	109
Furst, Susan Beth	73
G.Bernth, John	122
Galasso, William Scott	24
Galko, Michael J.	58
Gallagher, CE	68
Garcia, Dianne	127
Gargiulo, Marita	34
Geltrude, Daniel J.	109
George, Barry	72
Gilbertson, John S.	41
Gilliland, Robert	138
Giorgis, Joette	91
Glander, Scott	19
Godwin, Susan	55
Gonzales, Merrill	67
Goodman, Brent	110
Gorman, LeRoy	22
Gottlieb, Bill	126
Graetz, Carolyn Noah	17
Grandstaff, Sari	100
Green, John S	78
Greene, Steven H.	84
Greenhut, Frances	15
Grotke, Rob	87
Grover, Dana	6
Guenin, Anita Curran	52
Hafernik, Johnnie Johnson	63
Haggerty, Maureen Lanagan	72
Hahney, Tom	129
Hambrick, Jennifer	92
Han, John J.	20
Hanrahan, Mary	71
Hansel, Bryan	13
Harmon, Charles	12
Harrison, Devin	121
Harvey, Patricia	46
Harvey, Michele L.	103
Haslett, Arch	87

Hatter, Shasta	29		Koch, Dianne,	105
Hawk, John	106		Koen, Deb	5
Hay, Barbara	13		Kolodji, Deborah P	121
Haynes, Tia	27		Kozubek, S.M.	101
Hazen, Elizabeth	62		LaMarsh, Ron	69
Hemingway, Aubry	93		Lange, Jill	108
Hendricks, Paul	135		Lanoue, David G.	20
Herman, Randall	65		larkspur, mark	74
Herold, Christopher	16		Laurie, Christina	9
Higgins, Frank	48		Laurila, Jim	28
Hinchee, Merle	52		Lee, Michael Henry	101
Hinderliter, Carolyn M.	7		Lee, William E. III	21
Hishikawa, Judith	53		Lempp, Brenda	45
Hitri, Mark	61		Libro, Antoinette	6
Holzer, Ruth	59		Lindquist, Kristen	38
Hooven, Frank	125		Liu, Lydia T.	19
Hotham, Gary	35		Liu, Chen-ou	78
Howard, Elizabeth	52		Lloyd, Cyndi	76
Hryciuk, Marshall	49		Londner, Renee	9
Huggett, Elinor Pihl	71		Longenecker, Gregory	85
Hutchison, Connie	76		Losak, Amy	102
Ison, Erica	92		Lott, Kendall	28
Jackofsky, Rick	48		Lucky, Bob	75
Jackofsky, Gil	111		Luke, E.	53
Jacobs, David	35		Lukstein, Janis Albright	75
Jacobson, Roberta Beach	22		Lynch, Doris	90
Jambor, Lynne	5		MacCulloch, Jone Rush	134
Johnson, Tami M.	76		Machmiller, Patricia J.	115
Johnston, Paulette Y.	28		Mackenzie, Sue	112
Jongman, Hans	80		Makino, Annette	33
Judge, Frank	53		Martens, Elizabeth	132
Kacian, Jim	83		Martin, Jeannie	59
Keim, Robert K	99		mathews, michael	20
Kelly, David J	8		Mathur, Manoj	26
Kelsey, Julie Bloss	78		McBreen, Gerald A.	14
Kendall, Mary	75		McClintock, Michael	69
Kilby, Howard Lee	107		McCracken, Wilma	90
Kindelberger, Roy	18		McCullough, Vicki	102
Kirby, Mariam	95		McDonald, Tanya	34
Kittner, Craig	66		McGill, Marci	113
kjmunro,	33		McGregor, Marietta	17

McKeon, Joe	130	Pillai, Madhuri	42
McLaughlin, Dorothy	46	Poe, Marian M.	131
McMullen, Jeffrey	91	Pohlmann, Donna	40
McNeill, Robert B	56	Poirier, Marion Alice	63
Meester, Connie R	104	Polette, Keith	25
Meister, Peter	12	Powell, Marilyn	36
Merrill, RaNae	85	Powell, Perry L.	50
Metzler, Sarah E.	23	Pray, Sandi	99
Moeller-Gaa, Ben	31	Prefontaine, Joan	49
Moffett, Matthew	118	Pretti, Sharon	114
Momoi, Beverly Acuff	65	Prince, C.J.	8
Montreuil, Mike	129	Prine, Patricia	84
Moore, Lenard D.	79	Proctor, Vanessa	132
Morrissey, Laurie D.	86	Quinnett, John	63
Muirhead, Marsh	120	Ragatz, Barth H.	90
Mumford, Leanne	74	Raine, Katherine	96
Newton, Peter	137	Rainwater, Holli	125
Niedzielska, Suzanne	107	Rawson, Ann	10
Niehoff, Patti	128	Reed, Dian Duchin	14
Nika	37	Reinbold, Joanne M.	120
Nolan, Patricia	116	Rhutasel-Jones, Sharon	56
O'Leary, Karen	38	Rickert, Bryan	60
Okazaki, Tadao	95	Rielly, Edward J.	32
Olinger, Ellen Grace	45	Roach, Michael	19
Oliveira, Bob	17	Robello, Joseph	118
Olson, Ken	98	Robinson, Jackie Maugh	18
Ortiz, Victor	93	Robinson, Chad Lee	69
Owen, Renée	119	Rogers, Patricia	80
Packer, Roland	67	Root-Bernstein, Michele	62
Painting, Tom	112	Ross, Bruce	66
Palka, Kathe L.	102	Roy, Raymond	26
Patten, David	86	Rozmus, Lidia	29
Paulson, James A.	80	Rudychev, Natalia L	61
Pauly, Bill	43	Runkin, Patricia McKernon	117
Pazera, Juliet Seer	124	Rutley, Margaret	25
Pearce, Jacquie	18	Sacramona, Tom	122
Peckham, Ellen	64	Sambangi, Srinivasa Rao	15
Penton, Ann M.	15	Samuels, Clarise	106
Perez, D	58	Santos, Bona M.	50
Pierides, Stella	73	Sateriale, Eileen	135
Piko, Gregory	138	Savich, Agnes Eva	64

Schaefer, Michelle	36	Terry, Angela	98
Schallberger, Judith Morrison	81	Thampatty, Padma	58
Schoenburg, Mike	125	Thiermann, Jennifer	32
Schopfer, Olivier	131	Tice, Richard	105
Schwader, Ann K.	110	Tiefenthal, Deanna	82
Schwerin, Dan	105	Ungar, Barbara	113
Shaw, Adelaide B.	5	Updike, Claudia	49
Shaw, Kendra E.	94	Vance, Judith M.	57
Sheffield, Michael	66	Veeraja R	36
Shiotani, Charlie	47	Walker, Marilyn Appl	115
Shires, Nancy	16	Wallace, Jason Scott	27
Skane, George	61	Wallihan, Diane	40
skrivseth, d w	108	Warther, Julie	25
Slesnick, Carole	79	Watson, Roger	54
Smith, Robin	55	Watts, Lew	37
Smith, K.O.	60	Weidensaul, Mary	45
Smith, Crystal Simone	129	Weiler, Mary	101
Snow, Barbara	133	Welch, Michael Dylan	137
Sola, Nicholas M.	134	Wenk-Harrison, Christine	72
Sondik, Sheila	39	Wentworth, Don	16
Sorrels, Robert	132	Wesoky, Sharon R.	85
spooner, susan	46	White, Robin	94
Stelzer, Skaidrite	114	Whitmire, Bob	6
Stepenoff, Bonnie	136	Wiggerman, Scott	100
Sterba, Carmen	34	Wilson, Kath Abela	40
Stevens, Kathryn J.	115	Wilson, Stephanie Lemmons	106
Stillman, Jeff	10	Wilson, Billie	111
Stinson, Mike	123	Wirth, Klaus-Dieter	13
Strange, Debbie	83	Witmer, Robert	134
Strong, Lee	82	Woerdehoff, Valorie Broadhurst	121
Sullivan, Jim	47	Won, James	32
Summers, Dean	57	Woolpert, Alison	123
Summers, Alan	119	Yarrow, Ruth	10
Sundaram, Sneha	135	Yee, Sharon Lynne	70
Swanson, Lesley Anne	93	Young, Karina M.	131
Swede, George	22	Zajkowski, Lori	30
Tabb, Steve	113	Zehner, Daniel A.	38
Tarquinio, Rick	67	Zimmerman, J.	97
Tassone, Frank J.	97		
Tate, Barbara	21		
Teaford, M. Franklyn	24		

www.ingramcontent.com/pod-product-compliance
Lightning Source LLC
Chambersburg PA
CBHW032036040426
42449CB00007B/910